حقوق كبار السن في الإسلام
THE RIGHTS OF
ELDERS
in Islam

❴SHAYKH 'ABDUR-RAZZAAQ BIN 'ABDIL-MUHSIN AL-'ABBAD AL-BADR❵

❴حفظه الله❵

ISBN: 978-1-4675-1882-6

First Edition, May 2012 C.E./Jumada Thani 1433 A.H.

Cover Design By: www.strictlysunnahdesigns.com

Printed by Ohio Printing

Translation by Abu Fouzaan Qaasim

Revision of Translation by Abu Sulaymaan Muhammad Abdul Azim Ibn Joshua Baker

Website: www.maktabatulirshad.com

Email: info@maktabatulirshad.com

Subject: Akhaalaq & Aadaab

TABLE OF CONTENTS

BRIEF BIOGRAPHY OF THE AUTHOR 4

PREFACE 7

REMINDER ABOUT RIGHTS 9

GAINING KNOWLEDGE ABOUT THE RIGHTS OF OTHERS IS AMONG THE MOST SIGNIFICANT OF OBLIGATIONS 11

THE STATUS OF MORAL CHARACTER IN THE LEGISLATION OF ISLAM 15

THE IMPORTANCE OF COMPREHENDING THE BEAUTIES OF ISLAM 18

THE RIGHTS OF THE ELDERS 24

TEXTUAL EVIDENCES FROM THE QUR'AN AND SUNNAH 36

THE IMPACT OF SERMONS AND REMINDERS SHOULD NOT BE TEMPORARY 37

DIRECTIVES THAT MUST BE ADHERED TO FOR THESE RIGHTS TO BE UPHELD 40

THE RIGHTS OF THE ELDERS 52

CONCLUSION 70

BRIEF BIOGRAPHY OF THE AUTHOR

His name: Shaykh 'Abdur-Razzaaq bin 'Abdil-Muhsin al-'Abbad al-Badr.

He is the son of Al-'Allamah Muhaddith of Medina Shaykh 'Abdul-Muhsin al-'Abbad al-Badr.

Birth: he was born on the 22nd day of Dhul-Qiddah in the year 1382 AH in Az-Zal'fi, Kingdom of Saudi Arabia. He currently resides in al-medina al-Muna warrah.

Current occupation: he is a member of the teaching staff in the Islamic University, in al-medina.

Scholastic certifications: doctorate in Aqeedah.

The Shaykh has authored books, researches, as well as numerous explanations in different sciences. Among them:

1. Fiqh of supplications & Ad-Dhkaar.

2. Hajj & refinement of souls,

3. Explanation of the book "exemplary principles" by Shaykh Uthaymeen (may Allaah have mercy upon him).

4. Explanation of the book "the principles of names & attributes" authored by Shaykh-ul-Islam Ibn Qayyum (may Allaah have mercy upon him).

5. Explanation of the book "good words" authored by Shaykh-ul-Islam Ibn Qayyum (may Allaah have mercy upon him).

6. Explanation of the book "aqeedah tahaawiyyah".

7. Explanation of the book "Fusuul: a biography of the Messenger ﷺ) by Ibn Katheer (may Allaah have mercy upon him).

8. He has a full explanation of the book "Aadaab-ul-Muf'rad" authored by Imam Bukhari (may Allaah have mercy upon him).

From the most distinguished scholars whom he has taken knowledge and acquired knowledge from are:

1. His father Al-'Allamah Shaykh 'Abdul-Muhsin al-Badr — may Allaah preserve him.

2. Al-'Allamah Shaykh Ibn Baaz — may Allaah have mercy upon him.

3. Al-'Allamah Shaykh Muhammad bin Saleh al-'Uthaymeen—may Allaah have mercy upon him.

4. Shaykh Ali Nasir Faqeehi—may Allaah preserve him.

PREFACE

I praise Allaah Al-*Kareem* (i.e. The generous) by all of what He is praised for which He is deserving of. I praise Him, the blessed and exalted, with abundant and good praises, with blessings just as our Lord loves and contented. I praise Him, the Glorious and Exalted, for what He gives, because of His benevolence, His blessings, and his merits. I praise Him, the glorious and most high, because He guided us to this tremendous religion, and he granted us to the ability to adhere to the *Sunnah* of His Noble Prophet—May Allaah send blessings and praise upon him. I praise Him, the glorious and high, for every blessing which He has bestowed upon us old or new, in secret or openly, specific or, in general, while living or after death, that which is seen or unseen. All the praise that pleases him belongs to him, and all the praise as long as He is pleased with it is his.

I testify that there is no deity worthy to be worshiped in truth except Allaah alone, who has no partners. Besides him, there are no other lords.

There is no other creator except He—the Mighty and Sublime. He is the true deity of the beginning and ending of creation. He is the establisher and Sustainer of the heavens and the earth. He is the creator of all of creation.

I testify that Muhammad is His Servant, Messenger, His chosen friend, and His *Khaleel* (i.e., His exclusive and faithful companion). He is the custodian of His revelation. He is the one who conveyed Allaah's legislation to mankind. He left his nation on a clear path; its night is like its day. No person deviates from it after him (the coming of the Prophet ﷺ) except that he is destroyed. He established the proof (that will be for or against man). He clarified the way and explained the path. He did not go over any good except that he directed his Ummah to it. He did not go over any evil except that he warned his Ummah from it. He fought and strove in the path of Allaah rightfully so until death came to him.

May Allaah's Salat (i.e. His praise and blessings), His angels Salat, His Prophets Salat, and the righteous among His servants Salat be bestowed upon him.

As to proceed:

Indeed, the Muslims today are in a dire need of being reminded of the rights of Allaah, the Mighty and Majestic, the rights of His Messenger ﷺ , the rights of parents, relatives, neighbors, elders, and so forth regarding rights.

REMINDER ABOUT RIGHTS

Reminding the Muslims about these rights is a portal to good and a path towards righteousness and prosperity. So when the Muslim is reminded, he takes heed, and when he is directed to good then he is led on the right way. Allaah says,

$$﴿ وَذَكِّرْ فَإِنَّ ٱلذِّكْرَىٰ نَفَعُ ٱلْمُؤْمِنِينَ ۝ ﴾$$

"And remind (by preaching the Qur'ân, O Muhammad) for verily, the reminding profits the believers." [*Soorah Adh-Dhariyat* 51:55]

So the Muslim can recognize the beauty of this blessed legislation is the legislation of Islam. And that this religion is the religion of justice, the religion of giving everyone their due rights respectively, as Allaah says,

$$﴿ ۞ إِنَّ ٱللَّهَ يَأْمُرُ بِٱلْعَدْلِ وَٱلْإِحْسَـٰنِ وَإِيتَآئِ ذِى ٱلْقُرْبَىٰ وَيَنْهَىٰ عَنِ ٱلْفَحْشَآءِ وَٱلْمُنكَرِ وَٱلْبَغْىِ يَعِظُكُمْ لَعَلَّكُمْ تَذَكَّرُونَ ۝ ﴾$$

"Verily, Allaah enjoins Al-Adl (i.e., Justice and worshipping none but Allaah Alone - Islamic

Monotheism) and Al-Ihsân i.e., To be patient in performing your duties to Allaah, totally for Allaah's sake and in accordance with the Sunnah (legal ways) of the Prophet in a perfect manner], and giving (help) to kith and kin i.e., All that Allaah has ordered you to give them e.g., Wealth, visiting, looking after them, or any other help, etc.: And forbids Al-Fahshâ' (i.e. All evil deeds, e.g. Illegal sexual acts, disobedience of parents, polytheism, to tell lies, to give false witness, to kill a life without right, etc.), And Al-Munkar i.e., All that is prohibited by Islamic law: polytheism of every kind, disbelief and every type of evil deed, etc., And Al-Baghy (i.e. All types of oppression), He admonishes you, that you may take heed." [*Soorah An-Nahl* 16:90]

As a result, the establishment of these rights has been given to the Muslim since the person who lacks in a matter cannot give it. Thus, the one who does not know the rights of Allaah that are upon him, or rights of the Messenger, the rights of parents, the rights of neighbors, or the elderly in Islam and so forth, then how could he possibly establish their rights? How can he possibly be just?

GAINING KNOWLEDGE ABOUT THE RIGHTS OF OTHERS IS AMONG THE MOST SIGNIFICANT OF OBLIGATIONS

Because of this, it is from the most important of matters and most emphasized obligations is to be concerned with learning the rights of others; And that the Muslim's concern about the rights, and learning about them should be with the intention of performing it and establish it in an accurate and complete manner.

It is a must also to implement it as an act of worship to Allaah alone; seeking nearness to Him. This knowledge should not be merely to obtain information, to grow in knowledge and have a wealth of experience and so forth.

So this is not the intention of knowledge; rather, the only purpose of learning is to act upon it. This is the reason Ali Bin Abi Taalib, may Allaah be pleased with him, said:

يَهْتِفُ الْعِلْمُ بِالْعَمَلِ، فَإِنْ أَجَابَهُ وَ إِلَّا ارْتَحَلَ

"Knowledge invites to carry it out. If he response to its request then it will remain, and if not it will depart." [1]

Thus, the circumstance will not be free from this knowledge either being a proof for or against you; a proof for you if your concern is to apply what you have heard, and you have implemented what you have been guided to of goodness, truth, and what is right, or it could be a proof against you if your pleasure from these sciences and learning is simply having a reputation. As the Messenger of Allaah ﷺ had said,

وَالْقُرْآنُ حُجَّةٌ لَكَ أَوْ عَلَيْكَ

"The Quran will be a proof for you, or against you." [2]

This requires all of us to have, within our hearts, a pure intention between ourselves and Allaah pertaining to our listening to these rights in intending to carry them out, as well as performing and completing them.

---

[1] **Translator's Notes:** Meaning if one does not act upon his knowledge then it will not remain with him. Look in the book "jaami' bayaan". Al-Khateeb al-Baghdadi noted it in the book "Knowledge mandates action" #40.

[2] Muslim noted it (#328).

So as a result, he should listen closely, and he should have a prepared mind for acting according to them. He should not have in his mind to be disinclined, *mutraakhiyah*[3], or *mutawaaniyah*[4]. For indeed the likes of this will not benefit.

Because of this we are in greater need of these two affairs that Ibn Qayyim al-Jowziyyah (May Allaah have mercy upon him) has mentioned in his book *Miftaah Daar Sa'aadah* [5] to what we could become in the example of this situation where he stated:

"The perfection of every person can only be accomplished by these two qualities:

Ardent determination that will elevate and raise him

And Knowledge that will give him insight and guide him.

Hence, indeed the degrees of happiness and salvation will only escape from the servant from these two areas or one of the two. Either the person does not possess the knowledge about the degrees of happiness and salvation

---

[3] **Translator's note**: *"Mu'jaam al-Waseet"* (page 349) said this word means: one who does not hasten to have precision, and does not have a concern about a matter.

[4] **Translator's note**: *"Mu'jaam al-Waseet"* (page 1102) said this word means: to be languish, hesitate, and slow.

[5] Volume 1 page 46.

so he does not move with vigor in the pursuit of it. Or he is knowledgeable about it; however his determination does not embark upon it."

Hence, these are two affairs from the most significant affairs of what he should become:

- Knowledge that will guide you to the path of truth and what is right

- And a lofty goal that will exalt you. That is to say, it elevates you in the pathways to good and routes towards excellence.

If the person possesses knowledge but has no ambition in acting according to it, then his knowledge will be a proof against him. If he has a high purpose without any knowledge, he will carry out all matters haphazardly and rashly.

Therefore, just as we are in need of beneficial knowledge indeed we are also in need of high ambitions that, on the basis of it, the person will carry out the fulfillment of these obligatory rights and imperative duties which are upon every Muslim—male and female.

THE STATUS OF MORAL CHARACTER IN THE LEGISLATION OF ISLAM

Indeed from the beauty of our noble legislation is that it has brought noble and high characteristics out, and it has cautioned us from shameful and poor characteristics. He ﷺ said,

إِنَّمَا بُعِثْتُ لِأُتَمِّمَ صَالِحَ الْأَخْلَاقِ

"Verily I have been only sent to perfect and complete, righteous characteristics." [6]

And He ﷺ said,

إِنَّ مِنْ أَحَبِّكُمْ إِلَيَّ ، وَ أَقْرَبِكُمْ مِنِّي مَجْلِسًا
يَـوْمَ الْقِيَامَةِ أَحَاسِنَكُمْ أَخْلَاقًا .

"Indeed the dearest to me amongst you and the nearest companion to me on the day of

---

[6] Imam Ahmad noted it #8952, al-Bukhari noted it in *"Adab Mufrad"* #273 from the hadith of Abi Hurairah — may Allah be pleased with him. Shaykh Al-Albaani authenticated it in the book *"Saheeh of Adab Mufrad"*.

resurrection are those among you who are best in characteristics." [7]

Also, He ﷺ said,

إِنَّ الْمُؤْمِنَ لَيُدْرِكُ بِحُسْنِ خُلُقِهِ دَرَجَةَ الصَّائِمِ الْقَائِمِ .

"Indeed the believer will surely attain the level of the person who fasts and stands in the night (i.e., Praying at night) due to his excellence character." [8]

Therefore, the excellent moral character is among the things that this legislation invites to. So it invites to impeccable manners and noble character with Allaah, the Messenger of Allaah ﷺ, as well as Allaah's servants. They are blessed ways, and noble characteristics that the strength of this religion, its perfection, its completeness, and its high standing makes clear. That it is a religion of good qualities concerning its creed, its acts of worship, as well as its mannerisms and characteristics.

---

[7] At-Tirmidhi noted it #1941 from the hadith of Jabir — may Allaah be pleased with him. And Shaykh Al-Albaani said in *"Saheeh-ul-Jaami"* #2201 it is *Hasan*.

[8] Imam Ahmad noted it #25013, Abu Dawud noted it #4165 from the hadith of 'Ayesha — may Allah be pleased with her. And Shaykh Al-Albaani authenticated it in *"Saheeh-ul-Targheeb wal-Tarheeb"* #2643.

This matter since some of the Muslims — or perhaps many of them — have forsaken it the remnant of the peoples' interest in this religion has become weak from this angle. Otherwise, if the People of *Eemaan* were to carry out what their religion calls them to do pertaining to rights, obligations, etiquettes, and virtues in the best manner; and these characteristics were to emerge within them, and if these attributes had become evident then certainly this it is among the greatest avenues of inviting those to enter this religion.

THE IMPORTANCE OF COMPREHENDING THE BEAUTIES OF ISLAM

Indeed a time had long passed upon the Ummah of Islam when people use to enter the religion of Allaah in crowds and groups on the part of what they saw on the people of religion from the completeness of their morals, the beauty of their social graces, and the integrity of their social interaction in all aspects.

I read a statement of the great scholar, 'Abdul 'Azeez Ibn Baaz, may Allaah have mercy upon him and give him a place in paradise, in which he swore by Allaah, and he said:

الْمُسْلِمُونَ الْيَوْمَ ، بَلْ الْعَالَمُ كُلُّهُ فِي أَشَدِّ الْـحَـاجَـةِ إِلَى بَيَانِ دِينِ الله ، وَ إِظْهَارِ مَحَاسِنِهِ ، وَ بَيَانِ حَقِيقَتِهِ ، وَ الله لَوْ عَرَفَهُ النَّاسُ الْيَوْمَ ، وَ لَـوْ عَرَفَهُ الْعَالَمُ عَلَى حَقِيقَتِهِ

لَدَخَـلُـوا فِيهِ أَفْوَاجًا الْيَـوْمَ كَـمَا دَخَـلُـوا فِيهِ
أَفْواجًا بَعْدَمَا فَتَحَ اللهُ عَـلَى نَبِيِّهِ مَكَّـةَ - عَـلَيْهِ
الـصَّـلَاةُ وَ الـسَّـلَامُ .

"The Muslims today, rather the whole world, are in a more acute need of a clarification of Allaah's religion, an indication of its good qualities, and an explanation of its reality. I swear by Allaah if the people and the world actually knew its reality today indeed they would have entered it in multitudes, just like they came into in multitudes after Allaah had granted victory to the His Prophet ﷺ over Makkah." [9]

By Allaah, he proved to be true, and he was sincere. I met a man from India whom more than a thousand Hindus accepted Islam by his efforts. All of them accepted Islam one at a time; he did not give Da'wah[10] to two people together. His Da'wah only pertained to a single person.

His strategy in giving Da'wah was that he had excellent knowledge of the religion's good qualities, good manners, and its perfection. So whenever he encountered one of the Hindus—and in most cases, he would choose whomever he noticed had anxiety,

---

[9] Shaykh Ibn Baaz's Collection of Fatawa volume #2 page 338.
[10] **Translator's note:** meaning calling to the religion of Islam

grief, or regret about what passed him by, or he noticed that he was in a difficult sitting by himself. He would sit with him and ask him about his circumstance and his problem. There, he would mention to him some of the beauties of the religion. And he[11] said to me:

> **"For many of them, it would only take fifteen minutes, or half hour at the most. I would cite to him some good qualities of this religion. Afterward, he would ask me, "How do I enter this religion? What is the way so I can become one of the Muslims? How can I become a Muslim? So I demonstrated to him Islam (what to say to the two testimonies), and he embraced Islam."**

Indeed we — O nation of Islam, nation of Muhammad ﷺ is in great need of firstly knowing the good qualities of our religion, drink from its sweet spring and its natural spring well.

We need to seek its shade and quench our thirst from its fresh, pure water.

Therefore, we should follow Islam's moral examples. We should devote our attention to the good qualities which the Lord of all that exists has called us to. We should be conscious that these good characteristics

---

[11] The man from India who is telling the story to the Shaykh.

are a command that the creator of this universe and the Lord of all that exists, the All-Wise, All-Knowing ﷻ of his creation have called us.

Therefore, we should carry out his command, comply with it, submit, and obey hoping by that our Lord's reward and His generous promises to those who fulfill what Allaah commanded (us) to do the rights and obligations.

It is a must that you pay attention to this matter that your carrying out of these rights and your execution of them are only an act of obedience to Allaah, seeking Allaah's reward and waiting for His promises in this life and the hereafter. From His rewards, which are given in Dunya' and Hisﷻ blessings, which are provided in the hereafter, Allaah says:

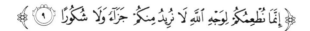

"(Saying): "We feed you seeking Allaah's Countenance only. We wish for no reward, nor thanks from you." [*Soorah Al-Insan*76:9]

So take heed that you do not give, in acts of kindness, anything unless you are compensated. If someone keeps ties with you, then you maintain relationships with them, and if they separate it then you do too. One of the companions said to the Prophet ﷺ :

يَا رَسُولَ اللهِ ! إِنَّ لِي قَرَابَةً أَصِلُهُمْ وَ يَقْطَعُونِي ، وَ
أُحْسِنُ إِلَيْهِمْ وَ يُسِيئُونَ إِلَيَّ ، وَ أَحْلُمُ عَنْهُمْ وَ
يَجْهَلُونَ عَلَيَّ

"O Messenger of Allaah, Indeed I have relatives, with whom I try to keep in touch with, but they cut me off; I treat them well, but they abuse me; I am patient and kind towards them, but they behave in a foolish way towards me."

So the Messenger ﷺ did not instruct him to sever his relationship with them although they would do so with him.

He ﷺ only told him to keep the ties of kinship even though they may break them, and he reminded him of the reward of Allaah and His magnificent favors. Then He, said:

لَئِنْ كُنْتَ كَمَا قُلْتَ ، فَكَأَنَّمَا تُسِفُّهُمُ الْمَلَّ ،
وَ لَا يَزَالُ مَعَكَ مِنَ اللهِ ظَهِيرٌ عَلَيْهِمْ مَا دُمْتَ
عَلَى ذَلِكَ .

"If you are as you say, then it is as if you are putting medicinal powder on their faces.

Allaah will continue to assist you as long as you continue to do that." 12

We come to the point that follows this introduction subsequently. For indeed among these tremendous rights that this real religion calls and invites to are *the rights of elders.*

---

12 Muslim reported it #6440 from the hadith of Abi Hurairah, may Allaah be pleased with him.

THE RIGHTS OF THE ELDERS

Whether this elder is a father, a relative, a neighbor, a Muslim or a non-Muslim the elder has a right that the legislation of Islam has come to keep, protect and establish.

It was mentioned in an authentic narration from the Prophet ﷺ, from the hadith of Abi Musa' al-Ash'ari ؓ that the Messenger of Allaah ﷺ said:

إِنَّ مِنْ إِجْلَالِ اللهِ إِكْرَامَ ذِي الشَّيْبَةِ الْمُسْلِمِ ، وَ حَامِلِ الْقُرْآنِ غَيْرِ الْغَالِي فِيهِ وَ الْجَافِي عَنْهُ ، وَ إِكْرَامَ ذِي السُّلْطَانِ الْمُقْسِطِ .

"Indeed from having reverence for Allaah is to respect the white- headed (elderly) Muslim, the one who memorized the Quran, who does not abandon reciting it nor is he extreme in it; and the one who rules justly. " [13]

Therefore, these three individuals honoring them is from the signs of having reverence for Allaah ﷻ and admiration of Him ﷻ, is the most magnificent demand and most glorious of goals.

---

[13] Abu Dawud noted it #4843. And Shaykh Al-Albaani graded it to be *Hasan* in his book *"Saheeh-ul-Jaami"* #2199.

The neglectfulness of this obligation is a disregard of Allaah's admiration. Because, the Lord of all that exists invites you to do this matter due to what it contains of good, benefit, excellence, perfection, and beauty. So if, you negligent this, then your neglectfulness is a weakness in your establishment of the reverence of the Lord of all that exists. Your establishment of this respect is from your reverence to the Lord of all that exists.

So direct your attention to this lofty status and exalted station, which this right has established that it is a right of the old, grey-haired Muslim; rather, it is established in the authentic hadith that our Prophet ﷺ said,

لَيْسَ مِنَّا مَنْ لَمْ يُوَقِّرْ كَبِيرَنَا وَ يَرْحَمْ صَغِيرَنَا

"He is not from us whoever does not respect our elders and shows mercy to our young." [14]

Therefore, the elderly deserve respect and honor. They have a position, rank, and prestige that are imperative that it is preserved and maintained. So whoever does not respect the elders then he is not from us. The Prophet's ﷺ , statement:

---

[14] At-Tirmidhi noted it #1842 from the hadith of Anas, may Allaah be pleased with him. And it is in the book *"Saheehah"* of Shaykh Al-Albaani #2196.

لَيْسَ مِنَّا

"Not from us."

Pertaining to the (above statement) is that whoever does not respect the elder and honor him is not upon the guidance of the Prophet ﷺ nor is he upon his proper way or His *Sunnah*, may peace be upon him.

Indeed, this right with respect to what it is surrounded by it becomes greater and gains more importance.

If he is a relative, then he has the right of kinship along with the right being elderly. If he is a neighbor, then, in addition, to his right of being an elder, is his right of being a neighbor.

If he is a Muslim, then he has the right of Islam along with his right of being elderly. If the elder is a father or grandfather, then the right is greater. Even if the elderly person is non-Muslim, then he has the right of being elderly since the legislation has set out to safeguard the rights of the elderly even if he is among the non-Muslims.

So perhaps your adherence to his right could be a reason for him accepting this religion during this latter stage in his life and closeness to leaving this world.

So he will see the generosity, kindness, nobility, and beauty of this religion. Especially, if he sees that his rights are being neglected within his false creeds and the false belief that he was raised upon and lived.

Thus, he will enter into the religion based upon this shining matter that he sees with his own eyes whereas this right has been neglected.

So that has come in between him and accepting this religion, and this is an observation that it is essential to follow.

Let's ponder over this fantastic story that was collected by Imaam Ahmad in his *Musnad*[15]on the authority of Asmaa' Bint Abi Bakr, May Allaah be pleased them. She said,

لَمَّا وَقَفَ رَسُولُ الله – صلى الله عليه و سلَّم – بِذِي طُوًى ، قَالَ أَبُو قُحَافَةَ لِابْنَةٍ لَهُ مِنْ أَصْغَرِ وَلَدِهِ : أَيْ بُنَيَّةُ ! اِظْهَرِي بِي عَلَى أَبِي قَبِيسٍ ، قَالَتْ : وَ قَدْ كُفَّ بَصَرُهُ ؟! قَالَتْ : فَأَشْرَفْتُ بِهِ عَلَيْهِ ، فَقَالَ : يَا بُنَيَّةُ ! مَاذَا تَرَيْنَ ؟ قَالَتْ : أَرَى سَوَادًا مُجْتَمِعًا ، قَالَ : تِلْكَ الْخَيْلُ ، قَالَتْ : وَ أَرَى

---

[15] #26956 and Shaykh Al-Albaani graded its chain of narrators to be *Hasan* in his book "As-Saheehah" volume #1, #895.

رَجُلًا يَسْعَى بَيْنَ ذَلِكَ السَّوَادِ مُقْبِلًا وَ مُدْبِرًا ، قَالَ : يَا بُنَيَّةُ ! ذَلِكَ الْوَازِعُ ، يَعْنِي الَّذِي يَأْمُرُ الْخَيْلَ وَ يَتَقَدَّمُ إِلَيْهَا ، ثُمَّ قَالَتْ : قَدْ وَ الله إِنْتَشَرَ السَّوَادُ ، فَقَالَ : قَدْ وَ الله إِذَا دَفَعَتِ الْخَيْلُ ، فَأَسْرِعِي بِي إِلَى بَيْتِي ، فَانْحَطَّتْ بِهِ ، وَ تَلَقَّاهُ الْخَيْلُ قَبْلَ أَنْ يَصِلَ إِلَى بَيْتِهِ ، وَ فِي عُنُقِ الْجَارِيَةِ طَوْقٌ لَهَا مِنْ وَرِقٍ ، فَتَلَقَّاهُ رَجُلٌ ، فَاقْتَلَعَهُ مِنْ عُنُقِهَا ، قَالَتْ : فَلَمَّا دَخَلَ رَسُولُ الله ـ صَلَّى الله عَلَيْهِ وَ سَلَّمَ مَكَّةَ ، وَ دَخَلَ الْمَسْجِدَ ، أَتَاهُ أَبُو بَكْرٍ بِأَبِيهِ ، فَلَمَّا رَآهُ رَسُولُ الله ـ صَلَّى الله عَلَيْهِ وَ سَلَّمَ ـ ، قَالَ : ((هَلَّا تَرَكْتَ الشَّيْخَ فِي بَيْتِهِ حَتَّى أَكُونَ أَنَا آتِيهِ فِيهِ)) ، قَالَ أَبُو بَكْرٍ : يَا رَسُولَ الله ! هُوَ أَحَقُّ أَنْ يَمْشِيَ إِلَيْكَ مِنْ أَنْ تَمْشِيَ أَنْتَ إِلَيْهِ ، قَالَ : فَأَجْلِسَهُ بَيْنَ يَدَيْهِ ، ثُمَّ مَسَحَ صَدَرَهُ ، ثُمَّ قَالَ لَهُ : أَسْلِمْ ، فَأَسْلَمَ ، وَ دَخَلَ بِهِ أَبُو بَكْرٍ عَلَى رَسُولِ الله ـ صَلَّى الله عَلَيْهِ وَ سَلَّمَ ـ وَ رَأْسُهُ كَأَنَّهُ

ثَغَامَةٌ ، فَقَالَ رَسُولُ الله – صَلَّى اللهُ عَلَيْهِ وَ سَلَّمَ
: ((غَيِّرُوا هَذَا مِنْ شَعْرِهِ)) ، ثُمَّ قَامَ أَبُو بَكَرٍ ،
فَأَخَذَ بِيَدِ أُخْتِهِ ، فَقَالَ : أَنْشُدُ بِالله وَ الْإِسْلَام
طَوْقَ أُخْتِي ، فَلَمْ يُجِبْهُ أَحَدٌ ، فَقَالَ : يَا أُخَيَّةُ !
اِحْتَسِبِي طَوْقَكِ))

"When the Messenger of Allaah ﷺ came to stop in Dbi Tuwa, Abu Quhaafah said to one of his granddaughters from his youngest son: "O little girl! Inform me of Abi Qabees." She said, "Indeed, he has become blind!?" She said, "So I had to watch over him." He said, "O little girl! What do you see? She said, "I see a crowd of people gathering." He said, "Those are the horses." She said, "I see a man moving in between the multitude from the rear and from in front." He said, "O little girl, that is the Wazii ". Meaning, he is the one who commands the horses and directs them. Afterward, she said, "By Allaah, the army has been spread out." So he said, "By Allaah when the horse moves then hasten me to my house. Then suddenly she was surrounded, and the men on the horses took him before he could reach his home. On the neck of the little girl was a necklace of hers made of paper leaves so a man reached for it and tore it from her neck she said, "So when the Messenger of Allaah ﷺ entered Mecca and entered the Masjid Abu Bakr brought Abi Quhaafah to him ﷺ.

So when the Messenger of Allaah ﷺ said to him, "Why did not you leave the old man in his house so that I could come to him in his house?" Abu Bakr said, "O Messenger of Allaah! It is more preferable that he walks to you than you walk to him." He said, "So he asked him to sit down in front of him."

Then he (i.e., The Messenger) wiped off the old man's chest and said to him, "Accept Islam and he agreed."

So Abu Bakr with Abu Quhaafah came to see the Messenger of Allaah ﷺ while his head (Abu Quhaafah) was like a tree/plant that has white flowers and fruits that can be compared to a grey haired person and the Messenger of Allaah ﷺ said: "Change this from his hair." Afterwards, Abu Bakr stood and took hold of the little girl's hand and said, "I request by Allaah for the necklace of my sister. And no one replied." So he said, "O my little sister! Please, sacrifice it in anticipation of Allaah's reward in the hereafter."

He, Imam Ahmad, noted it in summary from the hadith of Anas—May Allaah be pleased with him. And his wording,

لَوْ أَقْرَرْتُ الشَّيْخَ فِي بَيْتِهِ ، لَأَتَيْنَاهُ تَكْرُمَةً لِأَبِي بَكْرٍ

"Had you sat the old man in his house indeed we would have come to him out of honor for Abi Bakr."

What effect will this speech have on the soul? What impact will it have on the heart? By Allaah! It will indeed open the hearts full and will make it become accepted, and open hearted to what it is being invited to. So for this point he (the old man) rushed to embrace Islam without any hesitation.

Even if, a person's parents are non-Muslim, the legislation of Islam has brought the preservation of his rights out even if they call their son to disbelieve. The Most High says,

﴿ وَإِن جَٰهَدَاكَ عَلَىٰٓ أَن تُشۡرِكَ بِى مَا لَيۡسَ لَكَ بِهِۦ عِلۡمٌ فَلَا تُطِعۡهُمَاۖ وَصَاحِبۡهُمَا فِى ٱلدُّنۡيَا مَعۡرُوفٗاۖ ﴾

"But if they (both) strive with you to make you join in worship with me others that of which you have no knowledge, then obey them not,

[31]

but behave with them in the world kindly."
[*Soorah Luqmaan* 31:15]

He did not say,

"And if they strive to make you ascribe partners with Allaah with me others that of which you have no knowledge then be disrespectful to them."

Rather He said,

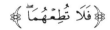

"Do not obey them."

Likewise, if the person's father abandons the prayer or is a *Faasiq* (open sinner) then his right of parenthood and his right of old-age remains. He should be treated according to the prerequisite of this right out of adhering to his rights and joining their hearts.

Perhaps Allaah will guide them back to the truth and what is right. At the same time, advice should be offered to him with good manners and without looking down upon him and being arrogant. Perhaps Allaah may bestow upon him guidance and success towards uprightness.

In any rate, our religion is a religion of goodness, ease, kindness, justice; it is a religion of adhering to the rights and carrying them out. It is a religion of giving every person his due rights.

Our legislation has come to safeguard the rights of elders and adhere to it even if he is not Muslim. So what is the case if this elder is a Muslim, a neighbor, a kin, or if he is a father or a mother? No doubt then the right is greater.

Rather, indeed this is from the greatest of actions that draw one closer to Allaah; from the most magnificent means of attaining Allaah's pleasure and relief from worries and facilitation of one's affairs just like what is witnessed in the story of the three individuals who took refuge in a cave in a mountain. So they entered it, and a boulder fell from the mountain and blocked them in the cave. Each one of them implored Allaah using his most virtuous actions. The *waseelah* of one of them was his establishment of this grand right and his adherence to this magnificent request where He said in his *Tawasul*,

اللَّهُمَّ ! كَانَ لِي أَبَوَانِ شَيْخَانِ كَبِيرَانِ ، وَ كُنْتُ لَا أَغْبِقُ قَبْلَهُمَا أَهْلًا ، وَ لَا مَالًا ، فَنَأَى بِي فِي طَلَبِ شَيْءٍ يَوْمًا ، فَلَمْ أُرِحْ عَلَيْهِمَا حَتَّى نَامَا فَحَلَبْتُ لَهُمَا غَبُوقَهُمَا فَوَجَدْتُهُمَا نَائِمَيْنِ

وَ كَرِهْتُ أَنْ أَغْبِقَ قَبْلَهُمَا أَهْلًا أَوْ مَالًا ،
فَلَبِثْتُ وَ الْقَدَحُ عَلَى يَدَيَّ أَنْتَظِرُ
اسْتِيقَاظَهُمَا حَتَّى بَرَقَ الْفَجْرُ ، فَاسْتَيْقَظَا
فَشَرِبَا غَبُوقَهُمَا ، اللَّهُمَّ ! إِنْ كُنْتُ فَعَلْتُ
ذَلِكَ ابْتِغَاءَ وَجْهِكَ فَفَرِّجْ عَنَّا مَا نَحْنُ فِيهِ مِنْ
هَـٰذِهِ الصَّـخْرَةِ

"O Allaah, I have two elderly parents, and I would give priority to no one over them two in drinking their share of milk, which they would drink. One day, I sought a matter that kept me distance (from the house), and I did not return to them until they had fell asleep. I milked the goats, cows of their afternoon milk, and I found them two sleeping (i.e., His parents). I disliked giving priority to anyone over them two in drinking their share of milk.

Thus, I remained while the drinking vessel was in my hands waiting for them to wake up at the appearance of Fajr. So they woke up, and they drank their afternoon milk. O Allaah! If I had done that seeking your face, then (please)

relieve us of what we are in pertaining to this rock." [16]

Therefore, that was a significant means of removing their worries, and it was a facilitation of their affairs.

---

[16] Bukhari noted it #2215 and 2272; and Muslim noted it #2743.

TEXTUAL EVIDENCES FROM THE QUR'AN AND SUNNAH

The texts of our purified legislation and evidences of the Book of Allaah and the *Sunnah* of the Prophet ﷺ in adhering to this right as well as establishing it are very abundant. The People of Knowledge have mentioned them in the books of manners.

If you were to read the superb book by Imaam al-Bukhaari, may Allaah have mercy upon him, *Al-Adab al-Mufrad* or other than that from the books of the people of knowledge in this area indeed you would see from the Prophetic narration as well as several texts, which call and invite the people of *Eemaan* and all of the Muslims to establish this grand right and preserve it; however, surely you would notice within this book as well as other than it from the books of the people of *Sunnah* the exalted decorum and sublime character with the elderly that the generation of the Companions۟ was upon as well as those who followed them in excellence.

So we will go through some brief instances of that as well as some reminders of it, Allaah willing.

THE IMPACT OF SERMONS AND REMINDERS SHOULD NOT BE TEMPORARY

At this point, we would accept a perspective that is required. If we were to hear about the rights of elders, the legislation's invitation to carry it out and adhere to it, then everyone of us will need of a summary of the things that every person should visualize within himself and has within his mind so that it will be an aid for him to carry out this task.

Otherwise, the influence of this hearing will be temporary or non-existent. I will mention briefly a problem that we are afflicted by it abundantly throughout our practical life whereas we certainly listen to beneficial lectures and impressive reminders except that our influence by it will be brief.

So to some people, the effects of the exhortation will stay with him for a week, or less, or more than it will come to a halt.

It is not appropriate for us that our circumstance is like this; rather, it is appropriate that our circumstance is that we are admonished and reminded from the ways of good is continuous and uninterrupted. Allaah, Most High, says:

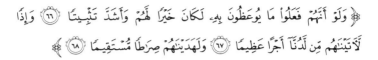

﴿ وَلَوۡ أَنَّهُمۡ فَعَلُواْ مَا يُوعَظُونَ بِهِۦ لَكَانَ خَيۡرٗا لَّهُمۡ وَأَشَدَّ تَثۡبِيتٗا ۝ وَإِذٗا لَّآتَيۡنَٰهُم مِّن لَّدُنَّآ أَجۡرًا عَظِيمٗا ۝ وَلَهَدَيۡنَٰهُمۡ صِرَٰطٗا مُّسۡتَقِيمٗا ۝ ﴾

"But if they had done what they were told, it would have been better for them, and would have strengthened their (Faith); and indeed we should then have bestowed upon them a great reward from Ourselves. And indeed we should have guided them to a Straight Way." [*Soorah An-Nisaa* 4:66-68]

From what is strange concerning what has been mentioned on this occasion is that one of the people who prays at the Masjid came to the *khateeb* [17] of the central *masjid* of his district scolding him, so he said to him:

"You have been preaching to us for several years, so what have you done? What thing have you sent forth??"

The *khateeb* responded to him without delay:

"And all during this time you have been listening carefully to me, so what have you all been doing??!"

---

[17] **Translator's note:** the khateeb is the one who delivers the Friday sermon.

Therefore, the duty of the *khateeb* is to clarify, admonish, and remind the people. The person listening should act according to the good whenever it reaches him and remain in it seeking assistance from Allaah in order that this good will stay him applying it in his actual life; continuously using it until Allaah calls him back while He, Allaah, is pleased with him.

DIRECTIVES THAT MUST BE ADHERED TO FOR THESE RIGHTS TO BE UPHELD

So on this topic that we are in *"The Rights of Elders in Islam"*, we are in need of matters which in brief are incumbent upon us to visualize within ourselves until it becomes an aid to us in establishing these rights; that we persist in applying them until we meet Allaah, the glorious and highest.

I hope to summarize them in some points:

The First point: Is that we stop at the textual evidences from the Qur'an and *Sunnah* that directs (us) to the importance of adhering to this magnificent right — the rights of elders. The evidences have a significant impact on upon the believing souls and sincere hearts. By Allaah! Then I swear by Allaah again! Indeed the statement of our Prophet ﷺ :

إِنَّ مِنْ إِجْلَالِ اللهِ إِكْرَامَ ذِي الشَّيْبَةِ الْمُسْلِمِ

"Indeed, from having reverence for Allaah is to respect the white- headed (elderly) Muslim."

If this statement had encountered a righteous heart, which does not have any opaqueness on it or anything covering it indeed it would cause the heart

[40]

to tremble and make an impression on it considerably. Likewise, his ﷺ statement:

لَيْسَ مِنَّا مَنْ لَمْ يُوَقِّرْ كَبِيرَنَا

"Whoever does not respect our adults is not from us." [18]

Therefore, we need to listen to these evidences, and these blessed narrations from our noble Prophet ﷺ so this listening will be an aid for us upon the good. Good has degrees and phases. So the first of its phases is listening, then comprehension, afterward action, and implementation.

Thus, these are the stages, upon which, the slave advances steadily. For this reason, the legislation has brought incitement towards seeking beneficial knowledge and sticking to its' gatherings, because it is the gateway, which the Muslim will take possession of moral excellence through all of its forms as well as good deeds from its most expansive gates.

The second point is that you seek assistance from Allaah and that you resort to Him﷾ in aiding you to carry out this right.

---

[18] Imam Ahmad noted it #6937, and At-Tirmidhi noted it #1920 from the hadith of 'Abdullah Bin 'Umar, May Allaah be pleased with them both. Shaykh Al-Albaani authenticated it in his book *"Saheeh-ul-Jaami"* #5444.

اِحْرِصْ عَلَى مَا يَنْفَعُكَ ، وَاسْتَعِنْ بِالله

" Be diligent in whatever benefits you and
seek the assistance of Allaah." [19]

And within the Noble Qur'an Allaah, the Most High
says,

﴿ إِيَّاكَ نَعْبُدُ وَإِيَّاكَ نَسْتَعِينُ ۝ ﴾

"You (Alone) we worship, and you (Alone) we
ask for help (for each and everything)." [Soorah
Al-Fatihah 1:5]

And Allaah ﷻ says,

﴿ فَاعْبُدْهُ وَتَوَكَّلْ عَلَيْهِ ﴾

"So worship Him (O Muhammad) and put
your trust in Him." [Soorah Hud 11:123]

Therefore, you do not possess any capacity to carry
out these rights except if Allaah provides you with
support and success granted by Him.

For this reason, the Prophet ﷺ said to Mu'aadh
Bin Jabal, may Allaah be pleased with him:

---

[19] Muslim noted it #2664 from the hadith of Abi Hurairah, May
Allah be pleased with him.

[42]

إِنِّي لَأُحِبُّكَ يَا مُعَاذُ ! فَقُلْتُ : وَ أَنَا أُحِبُّكَ يَا

رَسُولَ اللهِ ! فَقَالَ رَسُولُ اللهِ – صَلَّى اللهُ عَلَيْهِ وَ

سَلَّمَ : فَلَا تَدَعْ أَنْ تَقُولَ فِي دُبُرِ كُلِّ صَلَاةٍ : رَبِّ

أَعِنِّي عَلَى ذِكْرِكَ ، وَ شُكْرِكَ ، وَ حُسْنِ عِبَادَتِكَ .

"Verily, I love you, O Mu'aadh! So I said: And I love you, O Messenger of Allaah! Then the Messenger of Allaah ﷺ (May peace and blessings be upon him) said: "Do not forget to say at the end of each prayer: O Allaah--assist me to remember you, aid me to show gratitude to you, and assist me in worshipping you in a complete manner."[20]

So whenever you hear about moral excellence or one of the ways towards good, then you should ask Allaah to assist you upon that; that he facilitates it for you and that He grants you success to carry it out, and that He doesn't entrust you to yourself.

The third point: you, O Muslim, who has been granted success, should visualize the splendid results and universal good things that are adhering to this right and carrying it out in this life will result from you in the hereafter.

---

[20] Imam Ahmad noted it #22119, Abu Dawud noted it #1362, as well as An-Nisaaee' noted it #1303. And Shaykh Al-Albaani authenticated it in his book *"Saheeh-ul-Targheeb"* #1596.

DIRECTIVES THAT MUST BE ADHERED TO FOR
THESE RIGHTS TO BE UPHELD

Allaah, the Blessed and the Most High, has prepared for those who carry out these rights enormous good things and numerous blessings in their earthly life, as well as in their hereafter.

This kindness, good, and beneficence are among the means of having an abundance of provisions in this worldly life.

Also, the appointed time of the person is postponed, and he is blessed in his life. His troubles, distresses, sorrows are removed. The calamities and tribulations depart from him. He ﷺ, may peace be upon him, said:

إِنَّمَا تُنْصَرُونَ بِضُعَفَائِكُمْ

"You are granted assistance only by aiding the weak and feeble ones amongst you." [21]

He ﷺ said,

ابْغُونِي ضُعَفَاءَكُمْ ، فَإِنَّمَا تُرْزَقُونَ وَ تُنْصَرُونَ بِضُعَفَائِكُمْ

---

[21] Abu Nu'aym noted it his book *"Ma'rifa-tul-Sahaabah"* #577 from the hadith of Abu 'Ubaydah, May Allaah be pleased with him. And in its chain of narrations is Al-Waaqidee. Al-Bazzaar noted it #1159 from the hadith of Sa'd, May Allaah be pleased with him.

"Seek (by aiding) the weak ones among you, for you are given provision and support only because of your assistance to the poor." [22]

And He ﷺ said,

مَنْ سَرَّهُ أَنْ يُبْسَطَ لَهُ رِزْقُهُ ، أَوْ يُنْسَاَ لَهُ فِي أَثَرِهِ
فَلْيَصِلْ رَحِمَهُ

"He who desires adequate provisions and his life prolonged, should maintain good ties with his kith and kin." [23]

So if, the rights of elders is preserved, and the people of *Eemaan* (i.e., True faith) carry it out and adhere to it; then there is no doubt that this is among the greatest means of facilitation of affairs, immense blessings, and the removal of trials, tests and calamities from the people. Also, it is a reason for tremendous good and continuous benefits on the servant in his earthly life as well as his hereafter.

---

[22] Imam Ahmad noted it #21731, Abu Dawud noted it #2594, At-Tirmidhi noted it #1702, and An-Nisaaee noted it #3179 from the hadith of Abu Ad-Dar'daa', May Allaah be pleased with him. And Shaykh Al-Albaani authenticated it in his book *"As-Saheehah"* #780.

[23] Imam Bukhari noted it #2067 and Imam Muslim noted it #2557 from the hadith of Anas, May Allaah be pleased with him.

DIRECTIVES THAT MUST BE ADHERED TO FOR THESE RIGHTS TO BE UPHELD

The fourth point is that you bear in mind a principle and a fundamental law that many texts from Quran and *Sunnah* have directed to, verily it is:

$$كَمَا تَدِينُ تُدَانُ$$

"The way you treat others you will also be treated."

Allaah, the Sublime, and Most High said,

$$﴿ هَلْ جَزَآءُ ٱلْإِحْسَٰنِ إِلَّا ٱلْإِحْسَٰنُ ٦٠ ﴾$$

"Is there any reward for good other than good?" [*Soorah Ar-Rahman* 55:60]

And, on the other hand, He﷿ says:

$$﴿ ثُمَّ كَانَ عَٰقِبَةَ ٱلَّذِينَ أَسَٰٓـُٔوا۟ ٱلسُّوٓأَىٰٓ ﴾$$

"Then evil was the end of those who did evil." [*Soorah Ar-Rum* 30:10]

Hence, the reward for righteousness is nothing but righteousness and the reward for evil treatment results in harmful consequences.

For this reason, it is mentioned in a hadith, that is raised to the Prophet ﷺ -and within its *Sanad* (i.e., Chain of narrators) there is some talk about its authenticity — that He said,

مَنْ أَهَانَ ذَا شَيْبَةٍ لَمْ يَمُتْ حَتَّى يَبْعَثَ اللهُ عَلَيْهِ مَنْ يُهِينُ شَيْبَهُ إِذَا شَابَ .

"Whoever demeans/humiliates a person of old age will not die until Allaah brings forth someone who will degrade and humiliate him when he grows old." [24]

If you admire and fulfill the rights of His rights, then Allaah﷽ will facilitate for you those who will satisfy your rights in your old age as a reward for that which you used to do.

There will come a day, Allaah willing, where you will be aged, weak in the body, and senses. You will need

---

[24] Ibn Abi Ad-Dunya' noted it reporting it in the *"Lifespan and Old age"* #15. Pertaining to it (i.e. this narration) along with cutting off in the Sanad (i.e. chain) is the person named Ibraheem Bin Sarmah; Ibn Muayen said (about him) that he is a wicked compulsive liar. And it was mentioned from the hadith of Anas that was raised to the Prophet with the wording: "Not a single youth who treats hospitably a person of old age due to his age except that Allah will send to him one who will treat him hospitably in his old age." At-Tirmidhi noted it #2022, and Al-Bayhaqi in his book "the branches of Emaan" #10485, Shaykh Al-Albaani declared it to be "Mun'kar" in his book *"Ad-Daeefah"* #304.

those around you to take care of your rights and respect you.

So if, you were unmindful of that with those individuals in your youth then that will be the recompense for your actions.

كَمَا تَـدِيـنُ تُـدَانُ

"The way you treat others you will also be treated." [25]

This is a past and well known *Sunnah* (i.e., Way of things). The people are fully aware of their reality, and they have witnessed it within their selves as well as others. So it is upon the slave who is true to himself that he must have *Taqwaa* of Allaah﷾, carry out these rights, and observe them seeking His﷾ reward, virtues, favors, and kindness.

The fifth point: Is that you closely examine the blessed state that our Pious Predecessors were upon from manners amongst the elders, respecting them, and respecting, value, and carrying out their rights.

Therefore, you should notice that matter that our Pious Predecessors were upon. So if, you read the biographies; the biographies of the Companions and

---

[25] He, the Shaykh mentioned a hadith, however it is not authentic. Look in Shaykh Al-Albaani's book *"Daeefah"* #4510.

those who followed them in righteousness, you will find pleasant stories and sweet-scented tales that they experienced.

You will find that the youth from the companions and the *Taabieen* (the second generation of Muslims) were in the utmost degree of manners and utmost respect towards the elderly.

So you should learn noble mannerisms and noble characteristics through these biographies; however the one whose life passes him by and the splendor of his youth passes while he was enchanted with reading about athletes and different artists[26] or the likes of them, then it is not possible for him to become acquainted with these noble and notable characteristics that our Pious Predecessors, the first blessed group (of Muslims) were upon.

---

[26] **Footnote from the author**: "From the grave atrocities that have afflicted some of the youth is that they may have been raised by elders, however they are ignorant of their rights and consequently fail to fulfill them. Some may even insult or physically harm them. Therefore, it is imperative that these youth sincerely return back to Allaah by learning about the rights of the elders and how to uphold them in the proper manner. They must be conscious of Allaah when dealing with them before the opportunity passes them by. How many were negligent of the rights of an elderly relative who may have lived with him then he passed away and thus the youth was stricken with deep sorrow?"

So how greater is our obligation to read their stories so we can increase and grow from the good that they were upon?

وَ مَنْ كَانَ بِهِمْ أَشْبَهَ كَانَ ذَلِكَ فِيهِ أَكْمَلَ

"Whoever resembles them will be the most complete regarding it." [27]

How beautiful is the statement of the one who said,

كَرِّرْ عَلَيَّ حَدِيثَهُمْ يَا حَادِي

فَحَدِيثُهُمْ يُجْلِي الْفُؤَادَ الصَّادِي

"O Haadin, [28]repeat to me their stories, for their stories drives away the thirsty heart."

Among the examples and parables of that is what is mentioned in *Saheeh* al-Bukhari and Muslim on the authority of Ibn 'Umar, may Allaah be pleased with them both, He said:

The Messenger of Allaah ﷺ, may peace be upon him, said to his companions one day:

---

[27] Majmoo' Fatawa Volume #10, page 210.

[28] **Translator's Note:** the word "*Haadin*" is the one drives the camels by singing to them (i.e. caravan leader). Refer to the Arabic dictionary "Mu'jam Al-Waseet, 5th edition, page 167.

أَخْبِرُونِي عَنْ شَجَرَةٍ ، مَثَلُهَا مَثَلُ الْمُؤْمِنِ .
فَجَعَلَ الْقَوْمُ يَذْكُرُونَ شَجَرًا مِنْ شَجَرِ الْبَوَادِي
، قَالَ ابْنُ عُمَرَ : وَ أُلْقِيَ فِي نَفْسِي – أَوْ رُوعِي –
أَنَّهَا النَّخْلَةُ ، فَجَعَلْتُ أُرِيدُ أَنْ أَقُولَهَا ، فَإِذَا
أَسْنَانُ الْقَوْمِ ، فَأَهَابُ أَنْ أَتَكَلَّمَ ، فَلَمَّا سَكَتُوا
قَالَ رَسُولُ اللهِ – صَلَّى اللهُ عَلَيْهِ وَ سَلَّمَ : هِيَ
النَّخْلَةُ .

"Inform me of a tree that is similar to that of
the believer." So they began mentioning trees
from the desert area. Ibn 'Umar said: "It enter
my heart—or my mind—verily it was the date
palm tree and I started to want to say it then all
of a sudden I noticed the age of the people, so I
was afraid to speak."

So once they became silent, the Messenger of
Allaah ﷺ, may peace be upon him, said:
"It is the date palm tree." [29]

The examples of that are abundant, and the
mentioning of some of them will come later.

---

[29] Bukhari noted it (21/ 6122) and Muslim (2811).

THE RIGHTS OF THE ELDERS

As for the rights of elders which Islam has invited us to and commanded (us) with are:

Firstly: Is honoring them just as it is mentioned in the hadith (i.e. Prophetic tradition),

يُـوَقِّـرْ كَـبِـيـرَنَـا

"He is not from us whoever does not respect our elders..." [30]

This is a magnificent statement that comprises of significant and very high meanings. The elderly should be honored, and he has dignity among the people.

He has standing, respect, and honor in the hearts' of the people.

This is the starting point and supporting pillar for carrying out the rights of elders; because whoever does not respect his elders, and then it is not possible for him to perform their rights.

---

[30] The complete hadith was mentioned earlier.

Therefore, honoring them is their right, and it is at the same time a supporting pillar for carrying out the rest of their rights, as well as all of its obligations.

Honoring the elder is that there should be a level of respect and esteem for them in your heart, and you should understand his level, status, and position. For this is one of his rights.

Secondly: is what is mentioned in the other hadith, the hadith of Abu Musa al-Ash'ari, may Allaah be pleased with him, that the Prophet ﷺ, may peace be upon him, said:

إِنَّ مِنْ إِجْـلَالِ اللهِ إِكْرَامَ ذِي الـشَّـيْـبَـةِ الْـمُـسْـلِـمِ

"Indeed from having reverence for Allaah is to respect the white- headed (elderly) Muslim." [31]

Meaning: that you should treat him reverentially according to what this statement directs (us) to; meaning with pleasant speech, excellent interactions, friendly act of love and other than that from the illustrations of kindness.

---

[31] This hadith was previously mentioned.

Thirdly: is that you should start giving them the greetings of peace: As it is in the hadith (i.e. Prophetic tradition):

يُسَلِّمُ الصَّغِيرُ عَلَى الْكَبِيرِ ، وَ الرَّاكِبُ عَلَى الْمَاشِي

"The young should greet the elderly. And the rider should greet a pedestrian." [32]

Therefore, whenever you encounter a Muslim elder do not wait for him to greet you. Rather hurry and rush to give him the salutations of peace with all good manners, respect, and politeness.

Also, pay attention to his condition in his elderly age. So if, his hearing is still intact then you should greet him in a voice which he can hear, and it should not harm him. If because of his elderly age his hearing is burdensome then you should also take that into consideration.

Fourthly: Whenever you speak with an elder be sure to call him by the most gracious address like **"O Uncle"** or similar to that out of respect for his age, worth, and rank.

---

[32] Bukhari noted it (#6231-6232) and Muslim noted it #5772 from the hadith of Abi Hurairah — may Allaah be pleased with him.

On the authority of Abu Umaamah Bin Sahl, may Allaah be pleased with him, he said,

صَلَّيْنَا مَعَ عُمَرَ بْنِ عَبْدِ الْعَزِيزِ الظُّهْرَ ثُمَّ
خَرَجْنَا حَتَّى دَخَلْنَا عَلَى أَنَسِ بْنِ مَالِكٍ
فَوَجَدْنَاهُ يُصَلِّي الْعَصْرَ ، فَقُلْتُ : يَا عَمِّ ! مَا
هَذِهِ الصَّلَاةُ الَّتِي صَلَّيْتَ ؟ قَالَ : الْعَصْرُ ، وَ
هَذِهِ صَلَاةُ رَسُولِ الله – صَلَّى اللهُ عَلَيْهِ وَ سَلَّمَ –
الَّتِي كُنَّا نُصَلِّي مَعَهُ

"We offered the noon prayer along with 'Umar Bin 'Abdul 'Azeez, may Allaah have mercy upon him. After some time, we left and came upon Anas Bin Maalik, may Allaah be pleased with him, and found him praying the forenoon prayer. I said: "O dear Uncle! Which prayer have you offered?" He said: "The forenoon prayer and this is the time of the

Prayer of Allaah's Messenger, may peace be upon him, whom we used to pray with him." [33]

Also on the authority of 'Abdur Rahman Bin 'Ouf, may Allaah be pleased with him, said:

---

[33] Bukhari noted it #549 and Muslim noted it #623.

بَيْنَا أَنَا وَاقِفٌ فِي الصَّفِّ يَوْمَ بَدْرٍ نَظَرْتُ عَنْ
يَمِينِي وَ شِمَالِي ، فَإِذَا أَنَا بَيْنَ غُلَامَيْنِ مِنَ
الْأَنْصَارِ حَدِيثَةٍ أَسْنَانُهُمَا ، تَمَنَّيْتُ لَوْ كُنْتُ
بَيْنَ أَضْلَعِ مِنْهُمَا ، فَغَمَزَنِي أَحَدُهُمَا فَقَالَ :
يَا عَمِّ ! هَلْ تَعْرِفُ أَبَا جَهَلٍ؟ قَالَ : قُلْتُ : نَعَمْ
، وَ مَا حَاجَتُكَ إِلَيْهِ يَا ابْنَ أَخِي ؟! قَالَ : أُخْبِرْتُ
أَنَّهُ يَسُبُّ رَسُولَ الله – صَلَّى الله عَلَيْهِ – ، وَ الَّذِي
نَفْسِي بِيَدِهِ ، لَئِنْ رَأَيْتُهُ لَا يُفَارِقُ سَوَادِي سَوَادَهُ
حَتَّى يَمُوتَ الْأَعْجَلُ مِنَّا .

"While I was standing in the front line on the day of the battle of Badr, I looked to my right and left and suddenly there were two Ghulaam [34] from the Ansaar "Hadeeth As'naan" [35] and I wished that I had been stronger than them.

---

[34] **Translator's note:** the word "*Ghulaam*" means a person from the time of his birth up until his adolescence. And it is permissible to apply it to men. Refer to the Dictionary "*Mu'jaam Waseet*" 5th Edition page 683.

[35] **Translator's note:** Ibn Al-Atheer in his book "*An-Nihaaya*" said about this phrase: "it is a surname for young men and in the first stage of life." Refer to the publication of Daar-ul-Ibn-il-Jaw'zi, 4th edition, page 192.

One of them winked at me then said, "O Uncle, Do you know Abu Jahl." I said: "What is your concern with him O nephew?" He said: "I was informed that he curses and insults the Messenger of Allaah ﷺ. I swear by the one who my soul is in His hand if I see him, I not separate myself from him until one of us dies." [36]

Fifthly: is that he is given precedence in speaking, gatherings, food, and entering; for this is among their rights. For this reason, it is mentioned in *Saheeh* al-Bukhari, and Muslim on the authority of Sahl Bin Abi Hathma, may Allaah be pleased with him, said:

انْطَلَقَ عَبْدُ الله بْنُ سَهْلٍ وَ مُحَيِّصَةُ بْنُ مَسْعُودِ بْنِ زَيْدٍ إِلَى خَيْبَرَ - وَ هِيَ يَوْمَئِذٍ صُلْحٌ - ، فَتَفَرَّقَا، فَأَتَى مُحَيِّصَةُ إِلَى عَبْدِ الله بْنِ سَهْلٍ وَ هُوَ يَتَشَحَّطُ فِي دَمٍ قَتِيلًا ، فَدَفَنَهُ ، ثُمَّ قَدِمَ الْمَدِينَةَ فَانْطَلَقَ عَبْدُ الرَّحْمَنِ بْنُ سَهْلٍ وَ مُحَيِّصَةُ وَ حُوَيِّصَةُ ابْنَا مَسْعُودٍ إِلَى النَّبِيِّ - صَلَّى اللهُ عَلَيْهِ وَ سَلَّمَ ، فَذَهَبَ عَبْدُ الرَّحْمَنِ

---

[36] Bukhari noted it #3141 and Muslim noted it #1752.

يَتَكَلَّمُ ، فَقَالَ : كَبِّرْ كَبِّرْ ، وَ هُوَ أَحْدَثُ الْقَوْمِ ،
فَسَكَتَ ، فَتَكَلَّمَا ، فَقَالَ : أَ تَحْلِفُونَ وَ
تَسْتَحِقُّونَ قَاتِلَكُمْ ، أَوْ صَاحِبَكُمْ ؟ قَالُوا :
كَيْفَ نَحْلِفُ وَ لَمْ نَشْهَدْ ، وَ لَمْ نَرَ ؟! قَالَ :
فَتُبْرِيكُمْ يَهُودُ بِخَمْسِينَ ، فَقَالُوا : كَيْفَ
نَأْخُذُ أَيْمَانَ قَوْمٍ كُفَّارٍ ؟! فَعَقَلَهُ النَّبِيُّ - صَلَّى
اللهُ عَلَيْهِ وَ سَلَّمَ - مِنْ عِنْدِهِ

"Abdullah Bin Sahl and Muhaiyisa Bin Ma's 'ud Bin Zayd set out to Khaibar. The inhabitants of which had a peace treaty with the Muslims at the time. They both separated and then Muhaiyisa came upon Abdullah bin Sahl while he thrown to the ground, trembling, wallowing in his blood. So He buried him and then he returned to Medinah. 'Abdur Rahman Bin Sahl, Muhaiyisa and Huwaiyisa, the two sons of Mas'ud rushed to the Prophet ﷺ. So Abdur Rahman began to talk, and then the Prophet ﷺ said, "Let the eldest speak" as Abdur Rahman was the youngest. So He, Abdur Rahman, kept quiet, and the other two spoke. The Prophet ﷺ (may peace and blessings be upon him) said: "If you swear as to who has committed the murder, you will have the right to take your right from the murderer. They said: "How should we swear if we did not witness the murder or see the murderer? The Prophet ﷺ (May peace and blessings be upon him) said; "Then the Jews can clear you from the charge by taking Al-Iymaan (an oath taken by men that it was not they who committed the murder)."

They said; "How should we believe in the oaths of Infidels?" So the Prophet ﷺ (May peace and blessings be upon him) himself paid the blood money of Abdullah." [37]

Also, the narration of the *Siwaak*[38]: and in other than that He ﷺ use to observe giving priority to the elder.

---

[37] [37] Bukhari #6655, #2937 and Muslim noted it #3160 from the hadith of Sahl Bin Abi Hathma, may Allaah be pleased with him.
[38] On the authority of Ibn 'Umar, may Allaah be pleased with them both, said: The Messenger of Allaah, may peace be upon him, said: "It was shown to me in a vision that I was rinsing my mouth with the *miswaak* and two people began to contend with each other over it. One was older than the other. I gave the *miswaak* to the younger one, but it was said to me: "Give it to the elder", so I gave it to the elder."

It is reported on the authority of Maalik Bin Maghool that he said:

كُنْتُ أَمْشِي مَعَ طَلْحَةَ بْنِ مُصْرِفٍ ، فَصِرْنَا إِلَى مُضِيقٍ فَتَقَدَّمَنِي ثُمَّ قَالَ لِي : ((لَوْ كُنْتُ أَعْلَمُ أَنَّكَ أَكْبَرُ مِنِّي بِيَوْمٍ مَا تَقَدَّمْتُكَ)).

"I was walking with Talha Bin Musrif, and we came to a narrow passage, and he would go ahead of me.

Afterwards, he said to me: "Had I known that you were older than me even by a day, I would not have gone ahead of you."

Also on the authority of Fadl Bin Musa (may Allaah have mercy upon him) said:

انْتَهَيْتُ أَنَا و عَبْدُ الله بْنُ الْمُبَارَكِ ، إِلَى قَنْطَرَةٍ ، فَقُلْتُ لَهُ : تَقَدَّمْ ، وَ قَالَ لِي : تَقَدَّمْ فَحَاسَبْتُهُ ، فَإِذَا أَنَا أَكْبَرُ مِنْهُ بِسِنَتَيْنِ .

"'Abdullah Bin Al-Mubarak, May Allaah have mercy upon him, and I came to an arched bridge so I told him to proceed.

He said to me: "You proceed." So I asked him his age, and I was two years older than him." [39]

Sixthly: is that you should observe their physical health, as well as, their mental state because of elderliness and frailty. This is among the matters, which many of the young are ignorant.

You should know that this stage, which he is living in, is a stage of total weakness in his body, health, as well as his senses; and if Allaah lengthens your life maybe you will pass through this point.

Mankind in the first part of his life and in the prime of his youth he is untouched, young, his body is docile and magnificent in appearance. Then he enters maturity of age so it changes his innate nature, and some of his strength dwindles. Afterward, he exceeds in age then he becomes elderly and older, lacking in strength, little movement, and incapable of performing the simplest of things. As Allaah says,

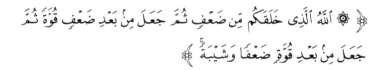

"Allaah is He who created you in (a state of) weakness, then gave you strength after weakness, then after strength gave (you) weakness and gray hair." [*Soorah Ar-Rum* 30:54]

And He says,

﴾ وَمِنكُم مَّن يُتَوَفَّىٰ وَمِنكُم مَّن يُرَدُّ إِلَىٰ أَرْذَلِ ٱلْعُمُرِ ﴿

"And among you there is he who dies (young), and among you there is he who is brought back to the miserable old age." [*Soorah Al-Hajj* 22:5]

Therefore, from his rights upon you are that you are aware of his physical circumstance, his mental condition, and senses; however, without a doubt some people because of their old-age, feebleness, frailty, and weaken senses, his dispositions and modes of behavior returns back to the nature of a young child, therefore, you must observe that.

Whereas the one who does not understand this matter, you will find him quick at becoming restless from what the elder does, and he becomes fed up with his (i.e., The elder) conduct; because he is not aware of the circumstance that the elder is undergoing.

So if, you envision this position, keep it in mind, and you will learn that it is a right upon you, and it is an obligation that requires that you adhere to it; then indeed you will carry out this duty, observe it in the perfect circumstance and in the most excellent of what it can be.

From the sad and grave matters is that some children carry out some of the good treatment in the initial stage. Then they get tired, weary and abandon the good treatment to the elder.

Rather, the matter enters a phase that some of the children take their father or mother to a place that takes care of elders, and they leave them in that location.

Rather, perhaps they disown them, turn away on their heels, and do not ever adhere to their rights except on visits. In some retirement homes, the father or mother remains there for fifteen years, less or more, and their children do not visit them even on the day of *Eid*. So if, this child was asked: **"Would you like for your kids to treat you like this when you become old?"** What will he say? Indeed he would be displeased with that for himself. And in the authentic hadith:

مَنْ أَحَبَّ أَنْ يُزَحْزَحَ عَنِ النَّارِ وَ يُدْخَلَ الْجَنَّةَ ،
فَلْتَأْتِهِ مَنِيَّتُهُ وَ هُوَ يُؤْمِنُ بِالله وَ الْيَوْمِ الْآخِرِ ،
وَلْيَأْتِ إِلَى النَّاسِ الَّذِي يُحِبُّ أَنْ يُؤْتَى إِلَيْهِ .

"Whoever wishes to be saved from the Fire and be entered into Paradise, then let death reach him while he believes in Allaah and the Last Day, and he should treat people the way he wishes for them to treat him." [40]

At any rate, regardless whether one of the parents reaches the level of senility or not, then carrying out their rights is imperative in exchange for their goodness towards you; you caring for them how they cared for you, and you protecting them how they protected you. Allaah says:

﴿ وَوَصَّيْنَا ٱلْإِنسَٰنَ بِوَٰلِدَيْهِ حَمَلَتْهُ أُمُّهُۥ وَهْنًا عَلَىٰ وَهْنٍ وَفِصَٰلُهُۥ فِى عَامَيْنِ أَنِ ٱشْكُرْ لِى وَلِوَٰلِدَيْكَ إِلَىَّ ٱلْمَصِيرُ ﴿١٤﴾ ﴾

"And we have enjoined on man (to be dutiful and good) to his parents. His mother bore him in weakness and hardship upon weakness and hardship, and his weaning is in two years give

---

[40] Muslim noted it #4882 from the hadith of 'Abdullah Bin Umaru — May Allaah be pleased with him.

thanks to me and to your parents, unto me is the final destination. [*Soorah Luqmaan* 31:14]

He, the Most High, coupled the right of parents with His right and gratitude to them along with gratitude to Him.

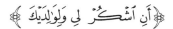

"Thanks to me and your parents."

This is an inseparable right that will last until their demise and Allaah will question the slave on the Day of Resurrection about that.

Seventhly: is supplicating for them, that you should ask Allaah to prolong their life in obedience of Allaah⌖. That you should supplicate to Him for them to be granted success and uprightness. That Allaah preserves them and grants them good health and well-being, and that He gives them a good ending. And that you should supplicate to Allaah that He makes them from amongst those whom the Messenger ⌖, said when he was asked about the best of people, he said:

مَنْ طَالَ عُمُرُهُ ، وَ حَسُنَ عَمَلُهُ

[65]

"Those who live the longest and perfect their actions." [41]

One said that Sulaymaan Bin Abdil-Maalik (may Allaah have mercy upon him) one day entered the mosque and found an old man. He greeted him and said:

يَا فُلَانُ ! تُحِبُّ أَنْ تَمُوتَ ؟ قَالَ : لَا ، قَالَ : وَ لِمَ ؟ قَالَ : ذَهَبَ الشَّبَابُ وَ شَرُّهُ ، وَ جَاءَ الْكِبَرُ وَ خَيْرُهُ ، فَأَنَا إِذَا قُمْتُ قُلْتُ : بِسْمِ الله ، وَ إِذَا قَعَدْتُ قُلْتُ : الْحَمْدُ لله ، فَأَنَا أُحِبُّ أَنْ يَبْقَى لِي هَذَا .

"O so and so, do you wish to depart from this life?" The elderly man replied in the negative. He said, "Why?" He said: "my youthfulness and its evil have departed, and the old- age and its good have arrived. When I stand up, I say, "In the name of Allaah." And when I sit, I say,

---

[41] Imam Ahmad noted it #17680-17698, At-Tirmidhi noted it #2251 from Ibn Basr. Imam noted it #20415, #20443, #20480, At-Tirmidhi #2252 from Abi Bakrah. And Shaykh Al-Albaani authenticated it in his book *"Saheeh-ul-Targheeb wal-Tarheeb"* #3364, and in his book *"As-Saheehah"* #1836.

"All praise belongs to Allaah." So I would like to stay in this condition." [42]

Meaning, that he wishes to continue being thankful, remindful and appreciative to Allaah. So the evil of his youthfulness and what it contains the overpowering of desires and leaning towards lowly things has passed. And now he has entered into the excellence and blessing of elderliness.

Therefore, he is living through the latter stages of his life nearing his departure from this world, so, he remembers Allaah, shows gratitude to him, and he praises Him, glorifies Him, says the statement of *Tawheed* (i.e., Laa Ilâha Illa Allaah) and supplicates to Him. Thus, he wants to stay in that state.

Eighthly: is that he (the person) knows that no matter how much he pays back his parents he will never amount to repay his parents. On the authority Abu Hurayrah, may Allaah be pleased with him, who said: "The Messenger of Allaah ﷺ, said:

لَا يَجْزِي وَلَدٌ وَالِدَهُ ، إِلَّا أَنْ يَجِدَهُ مَمْلُوكًا فَيَشْتَرِيَهُ فَيُعْتِقَهُ

---

[42] Ibn Abi Ad-Dunya' noted it in the book *"Al-'Umr wal-Sheeb"* #29, and Ibn 'Asaakir in the book *"Tareekh Damshaq"* #9159, and Ad-Deenuri in the book *"Al-Majalisah"* #2021.

"No son can repay the kindness shown by his father (parents) unless he finds him (i.e., His father) as a slave and buys him then free him." 43

And on the authority of Abu Burdah (May Allaah be pleased with him) said:

كَانَ ابْنُ عُمَرَ يَطُوفُ بِالْبَيْتِ فَرَأَى رَجُلًا يَطُوفُ حَامِلًا أُمَّهُ وَ هُوَ يَقُولُ :

إِنِّي لَهَا بَعِيرُهَا الْمُذَلَّل إِنْ أَذْعَرَتْ رِكَابَهَا لَمْ أَذْعَرْ أَحْمِلُهَا وَ مَا حَمَلَتْنِي أَكْثَرُ ، أُتَرَانِي يَا ابْنَ عُمَرَ ! جَزَيْتُهَا ؟ قَالَ : لَا ، وَ لَا زَفْرَةً وَاحِدَةً .

"Ibn 'Umar use to make circumambulation around the Sacred House in Makkah and he saw a man carrying his mother on his back saying: "I am like a tame camel for her! I have carried her more than she has carried me.

---

43 Muslim noted it #1510 in the book of *"Itq"* (freeing of a slave), At-Tirmidhi #1906 in the book of *"Al-Birr wal-Silah"*, Abu Dawud #5137 in the book of *"Al-Adab"*, Ibn Majah #3659 in the book of *"Al-Adab"*, and Imam Ahmad #2/230. At-Tirmidhi graded it is *"Hasan Saheeh"*.

Do you think that I have repaid her, O Ibn Umar? 'Abdullah Ibn 'Umar replied, "No by Allaah! Not even for the pain of one moan (from labor pains)!"

And on the authority of Al-Hasan,

أَنَّ ابْـنَ عُـمَـرَ رَأَى رَجُـلًا يَطُوفُ بِـالْبَيْـتِ حَـامِـلًا أُمَّـهُ وَ هُـوَ يَـقُـولُ لَـهَـا : أَ تُـرِينِـي جَـزَيـتُـكِ يَـا أُمَّـهْ؟ فَـقَـالَ ابْـنُ عُـمَـرَ : أَيْ لُكَـعُ ! لَا وَاللهِ ، وَ لَا طَـلْـقَـةً وَاحِـدَةً

"That Ibn 'Umar saw a man making circumambulation around the Ka'bah while carrying his mother and saying to her: "Do you think that I have repaid you O mother? So Ibn Umar said: "How foolish! No, I swear by Allaah that you have not even repaid her one time." [44]

Hence, these are in summary some of the rights that are mandatory that the Muslim must bear in mind in regards to those elderly, as well as some warnings and instructions concerning this glorious subject matter.

---

[44] Al-Mar'wazi noted both narrations in his book *"Al-Birr wal-Silah"* #37-38.

CONCLUSION

I ask Allaah to fill our gatherings with good and blessings; that He grants us success to acquire beneficial knowledge and righteous actions. I ask Allaah by His Beautiful Names and Lofty Attributes, that He blesses the elderly Muslims among our parents, relatives, neighbors as well as all the Muslims in general.

I ask Him to protect them, place them under His protection, and that He grants them a good ending, righteous actions and proper statements. Just as I ask Him to increase the blessings in this treatise, and that He makes it a blessed reason for uprightness and rectification. That He accepts it with a good acceptance, and that He makes it solely for His Noble Face, and that He makes it beneficial for His slaves.

Indeed, He is the All-Hearing of the supplications, He is deserving of all hope, and He is sufficient for us and the Best of Protectors and the end of our statements is that all praise is due to Allaah, the Lord of all the Worlds[45]

---

[45] **The Author's note:** the origin of this treatise was a lecture that I held in one of the Masajid in Jeddah. And it was transcribed from a tape. And I made some modifications and some additions. And I made a preface and a conclusion. So I preferred that it remained in the style of a speech just as it was in the lecture, and Allaah alone is the one who grants success.

Printed in Great Britain
by Amazon